SARAH AHNER

Google Pixel 9 Pro Fold User Guide

Learn how to Unlock the Full Potential of Your Android Device with This Step-by-Step Illustrated Manual Perfect for Beginners and Seniors

Copyright © 2024 by Sarah Ahner

All rights reserved. No part of this publication may be reproduced, stored or transmitted in any form or by any means, electronic, mechanical, photocopying, recording, scanning, or otherwise without written permission from the publisher. It is illegal to copy this book, post it to a website, or distribute it by any other means without permission.

First edition

This book was professionally typeset on Reedsy.
Find out more at reedsy.com

Contents

1 The Google Pixel 9 Pro Fold: An Overview ... 1
   Summary of Important Features ... 1
   Fold Series: What's New ... 2

2 Opening and First Configuration ... 4
   Opening the Item: What's Within ... 4
   Configuring the Pixel 9 Pro Fold ... 5
   Moving Information from Your Old Device ... 7

3 Hardware Overview and Device Layout ... 9
   Comprehending the Foldable Architecture ... 9
   Ports, Buttons, and Display Elements ... 11
   Using the Fold Mechanism Safely ... 12

4 Using the Pixel 9 Pro Fold to navigate Android 14 ... 14
   Basics of the Home Screen and Customization ... 14
   Quick Settings and Navigation Gestures ... 16
   Examining the Interface That Is Specific to Folding ... 18

5 Customizing Your Experience with Pixels ... 20
   Personalizing Wallpapers and Themes ... 20
   Configuring App Layouts and Widgets ... 22
   Handling Privacy Preferences and Notifications ... 23

6 Understanding the Camera System ... 25
   Triple Camera Setup Overview ... 25
   Using Extra Modes: Super Res Zoom, Night Sight, and More ... 26
   Guidelines for Getting the Greatest Pictures and Videos ... 28

7 AI Features & Google Assistant ... 30
   How to Configure and Use Google Assistant ... 30
   Smart Home Integration and Voice Commands ... 31

Using AI to Boost Entertainment and Productivity	33
8 Tools for Productivity and Multitasking	35
App Pairs and Split-Screen Modes	35
Making Use of the Recent Apps Menu and Taskbar	36
Making the Foldable Screen Great for Play and Work	38
9 Advanced Hints and Techniques	40
Developer Options and Hidden Features	40
Performance Enhancements and Battery Optimization	42
Making Effective Use of Gestures and Shortcuts	43
10 Features of Accessibility	46
Activating and Tailoring Accessibility Features	46
TalkBack, Magnification, and Voice Access	48
Device Optimization for Elderly and Handicapped Users	50
11 Maintenance and Troubleshooting	52
Typical Problems and Their Fixes	52
Taking Care of the Battery and Foldable Screen	54
Backing up and resetting your device	56
12 Commonly Asked Questions	58
Responses to Frequently Asked Questions	58
Guidelines for Optimizing Your Pixel 9 Pro Fold	61
13 Conclusion and Further Resources	63
Summary of Main Features and Advice	63
Helpful Resources & Additional Reading	66

1

The Google Pixel 9 Pro Fold: An Overview

Summary of Important Features

The world of cell phones has become somewhat predictable, let's face it. Slabs of metal and glass, each claiming to be somewhat quicker than the other or equipped with a marginally better camera. However, now and again something genuinely revolutionary happens to upend everything. Introducing the Google Pixel 9 Pro Fold, which is more than simply a phone; it's a doorway to an entirely new world of mobile possibilities.

Fundamentally, the Pixel 9 Pro Fold is evidence of Google's unwavering commitment to innovation. Its state-of-the-art Tensor G4 chip, a technological marvel that offers lightning-fast performance whether you're multitasking across several programs or losing yourself in the newest graphically demanding game, powers it. When combined with an ample 16GB of RAM, you'll encounter an unparalleled degree of smoothness and agility.

However, the Pixel 9 Pro Fold's innovative folding design is what makes it stand out. Imagine a gadget that, with a single unfurl, turns from a small, pocketable phone into an expansive tablet. The large 8-inch inner display opens up a world of possibilities for work, enjoyment, and creativity, while the 6.3-inch outer display is ideal for fast activities on the road. It can instantly adjust to your demands, almost like two gadgets in one.

A great camera system is a must for any Pixel phone, and the Pixel 9 Pro Fold delivers on that promise. With its triple-lens configuration, Google's well-known computational photography algorithms produce beautiful images and films in every lighting situation. Every picture, whether it be of a serene landscape or a close-up portrait, exudes brightness, clarity, and detail.

Not to mention the wonders of Google's artificial intelligence (AI): the Pixel 9 Pro Fold is intelligent, anticipating your requirements and simplifying your life in a myriad of ways. You'll be left wondering how you ever got by without it, with features like intelligent email suggestions and real-time translation into more than 100 languages.

Fold Series: What's New

The Pixel 9 Pro Fold represents a revolutionary breakthrough in folding technology, not merely a minor improvement. Google has spent many hours perfecting every part of the Fold experience while paying close attention to user input.

The hinge mechanism has been entirely redesigned; in previous folding devices, it was frequently a cause for concern. It guarantees a smooth, intuitive, and natural folding and unfolding experience because it's stronger, smoother, and more durable than before.

The screens have also seen a significant makeover, both inside and out. They now have increased brightness, vibrancy, and touch sensitivity. The visual fidelity and fluidity will captivate you whether you're creating your next masterpiece or just scrolling through social media.

One of the main advantages of foldable gadgets is that multitasking has been enhanced. Several new features and optimizations brought forward by the Pixel 9 Pro Fold allow multitasking with multiple apps and tasks easier than ever. You will discover that managing your digital environment is straightforward, from app pairing to split-screen mode.

Naturally, Google's AI powers are also developing at a dizzying rate. With even more potent AI functions, the Pixel 9 Pro Fold is sure to amaze and enchant you. You'll experience the convenience of having a personal assistant in your pocket with features like enhanced voice recognition and more logical contextual suggestions.

The Pixel 9 Pro Fold is essentially more than a phone. It's a declaration and proof of the infinite creativity of people. With this gadget, you can connect, explore, and create in ways you never would have imagined. It's the unfolding future.

2

Opening and First Configuration

When a new smartphone, like the Google Pixel 9 Pro Fold, is being unboxed, there's a mixture of excitement and intrigue. When you open the package, you're met with several lines, cutting-edge technology, and the prospect of novel experiences. This chapter will guide you through every step of the process, from setting up your Pixel to transferring data from your old device to what to expect inside the box.

Opening the Item: What's Within

It feels like you've entered a realm of precision and sleek design when you open the Google Pixel 9 Pro Fold package. Google's packaging immediately demonstrates its attention to detail. The small size and well-organized design of the box itself reflect the brand's emphasis on utility and simplicity. The contents are broken down as follows:

1. The Pixel 9 Pro Fold Device: Your Pixel 9 Pro Fold, the main attraction, is carefully positioned at the top of the package, encased in protective plastic. Despite being a foldable phone, the first thing you'll notice about it is how small and stylish it is. It's made to fit easily in your hand, but when you unfold it, you'll see a large, colorful display.

OPENING AND FIRST CONFIGURATION

2. Quick Start Guide: The quick start guide is located in a tiny booklet under the phone. This is a simple overview of the fundamental setup procedures, perfect for those who are unfamiliar with Pixel devices or Android in general.

3. USB-C Charging Cable: Google maintains its practice of providing a USB-C to USB-C charging cable, stressing its quick charging times and suitability for contemporary gadgets. The braided cable has a long lifespan since it is strong and made to resist abrasion.

4. SIM Ejector item: Nestled among the paperwork is this small but crucial item. When changing or inserting SIM cards, you'll need it to access the SIM card tray.

5. USB-C Adapter: Google comes with a USB-C adapter that makes data transfer across devices simple and works with previous charging infrastructure.

6. No Power Brick: The power brick is one obvious missing item. Assuming that customers already own wireless or suitable charging bricks, Google is adopting more environmentally friendly techniques, similar to many other contemporary smartphone makers.

Configuring the Pixel 9 Pro Fold

It's time to turn on your device now that it's out of the box. The Pixel 9 Pro Fold setup process is meant to be simple, especially for those who are not familiar with smartphones. To get started, just take these easy steps:

1. Powering On: Press and hold the phone's right-side power button until the Google logo shows up on the screen. The setup screen will appear as soon as the clear foldable display turns on. Here, you can connect to a Wi-Fi network and choose your chosen language.

2. Inserting the SIM Card: Use the SIM ejector tool to insert your SIM card before beginning the software setup. Find the SIM tray on the phone's side, slide the SIM card into it, and then slide the tray back in using the tool that fits into the little opening to release it. Later on in the procedure, you will be able to digitally configure your eSIM if you are utilizing one.

3. Google Account Setup: Google services are tightly integrated with the Pixel 9 Pro Fold. Make sure you sign in with your Google account to make the most of your phone. The setup process will walk you through making a new account if you don't already have one. Your Google account will facilitate a more seamless transfer by syncing your contacts, emails, apps, and settings from other devices.

4. Connecting to Wi-Fi: Make sure you're connected to a Wi-Fi network to install apps and download the most recent software updates. The gadget will look for adjacent networks on its own. Choose yours from the drop-down menu and input the passcode. At this point, Wi-Fi is essential to make sure you don't waste mobile data during the setup procedure.

5. Biometrics and Security: Google provides several options for protecting your Pixel 9 Pro Fold. A conventional PIN or password, fingerprint scanning, or facial recognition are your options. The handset's sophisticated front cameras guarantee quick and safe Face Unlock and a fingerprint sensor behind the screen offers another practical method of device unlocking.

6. Restoring applications and Data: The Pixel setup gives you the choice to restore contacts, applications, and data from your old device or a backup if you're switching from an iPhone or another Android phone. This process is streamlined by Google's data migration application, which works with both iOS and Android smartphones.

7. Google Services and Permissions: You'll be asked to activate several Google services during setup, including backups, Location Services, and

Google Assistant. Enabling most of these is a good idea because they improve your experience with voice commands, tailored services, and the ability to retrieve your device's data later.

8. Personalizing Your Device: After the setup is finished, your Pixel 9 Pro Fold will appear on the home screen. Here, you may begin customizing it. To make your phone feel unique, customize it with wallpapers, widgets, and app arrangements.

Moving Information from Your Old Device

Transferring all of your crucial data from your old phone to the new one is one of the most significant parts of setting it up. A few options are provided by Google Pixel 9 Pro Fold to guarantee a smooth data transfer procedure.

1. Using Quick Switch Adapter: Google's Quick Switch Adapter simplifies data transfer if you're moving from an older Android handset. Just use the USB-C adapter that comes in the package to connect the two devices, then adhere to the on-screen instructions. Everything is transferable, including contacts, messages, images, videos, and apps. The procedure is quick, effective, and safe.

2. Cloud Backup Transfer: The transfer goes even more smoothly for customers who use Google's cloud services. You may easily restore the backup that you created during the setup process if you were backing up your old device using Google Drive. Whether you're moving from an iPhone or an Android phone, this option is available. With a few taps, you can retrieve contacts, photos, apps, and even Wi-Fi settings from the cloud.

3. Moving from an iPhone: Google's setup procedure has been tailored to make room for iPhone users as well. With an iCloud account, you can transfer files wirelessly or straight from an iPhone via a cable. You'll be asked to go into your iCloud account during the Pixel setup process, where you can choose which information to transfer over, such as calendar events, contacts, messages, and images.

4. Manually Transferring Files: You can always manually move files from your previous smartphone to your Pixel 9 Pro Fold if you'd rather take a more hands-on approach. You can download crucial files from your old device onto your new Pixel by uploading them using online storage services like Dropbox or Google Drive. Alternatively, you can immediately transfer files between the two phones by connecting them to a computer.

5. Syncing Google Services: The majority of your Google apps, including Gmail, Calendar, and Photos, will begin automatically syncing data as soon as your new Pixel is configured. This guarantees that you won't miss a beat and can continue where you left off. For instance, as soon as you log in, your photographs from Google Photographs backups will display immediately on your new Pixel.

Your Pixel 9 Pro Fold will be operational and your previous data will have been securely moved to your new smartphone after following these procedures. Even if you've never set up a Pixel phone before, you won't have any trouble getting started because the entire process is made to be simple and effective. After everything is in place, you may start utilizing your foldable phone's potent new capabilities!

3

Hardware Overview and Device Layout

T he physical design, layout, and salient features of the Google Pixel 9 Pro Fold a marvel of contemporary smartphone engineering will be examined in this chapter. This folding gadget combines cutting-edge technology with user-centered design, marking a breakthrough in both functionality and aesthetics. Knowing your hardware is crucial to getting the most out of it, whether you're an experienced tech enthusiast or a novice.

Comprehending the Foldable Architecture

The newest model in Google's foldable series, the Pixel 9 Pro Fold, showcases the company's focus on combining functionality and style through its design. With foldable smartphones, consumers can now enjoy a larger screen in a more compact design, completely changing the smartphone business. The Pixel 9 Pro Fold is a symbol of versatility and innovation, but it's more than simply an amazing hinge.

The most noticeable thing about the gadget when you first take it up is how light and thin it feels, even with its dual-screen capability. When the phone is folded, it has a sleek, contemporary appearance and is small enough to fit easily in your hand or pocket. It unfolds to reveal a tablet-sized gadget with one of the largest displays available, making it perfect for reading, streaming videos, and multitasking. There is a level of versatility that regular smartphones just cannot match with this seamless transition between phone and tablet modes.

The device's display, which makes use of Super Actua Flex technology, guarantees that the inner screen is big, brilliant, vibrant, and fluid. The nearly bezel-less display offers an immersive experience when opened, enhancing the engagement of productivity programs as well as games. The screen can withstand thousands of folds and unfold without losing its sharpness or touch sensitivity because Google carefully considered every detail when designing it.

However, the fluid-friction hinge is what sets its folding design apart. The Pixel 9 Pro Fold opens and folds with precise, fluid motion, in contrast to certain previous folding devices from competitors that felt stiff or clumsy. The hinge holds firmly, preventing unintentional openings or closings, whether you open it halfway for a fast peek or fully for full use. The mechanism of the hinge has been tested to resist thousands of folds, contributing to the device's lifetime. This assures that the hinge can sustain years of use.

It goes beyond mechanics, though. Additionally, the foldable design is practical. Without having to fully open the phone, the external display makes it possible to perform fast tasks like checking notifications or replying to SMS. This guarantees that users can carry out tasks quickly and maintain battery life. For those who manage their personal and professional lives while on the go, the larger screen's internal ability to be divided into many windows allows for genuine multitasking.

HARDWARE OVERVIEW AND DEVICE LAYOUT

Ports, Buttons, and Display Elements

Understanding the buttons and ports arrangement is crucial to being a true pro at the Pixel 9 Pro Fold. Here's where the hardware excels, providing excellent build quality along with user-friendly controls.

The power button is located at the top of the gadget and is positioned to be easily accessed whether the phone is unfolded or folded. Additionally, fingerprint recognition is integrated into this button, enabling safe one-touch device unlocking. The location guarantees that the power button is always conveniently accessible, whether you're using the phone as a tablet or foldable device.

These volume controls are located next to the power button. Because of their small recessed appearance, Google makes it easy to distinguish them by feel. The buttons are comfortable and sensitive, allowing you to easily modify the audio during a call or make rapid adjustments while watching a movie.

The device's USB-C charging port is situated at its base. Due to its unusual construction, foldables are typically more difficult to design around charging ports; nevertheless, the Pixel 9 Pro Fold's connector is positioned thoughtfully for easy access, whether the device is folded or not. Even for the most discerning users, the device's support for wireless charging and fast charging guarantees that power will never be an issue.

Let's now discuss displays. The exterior display on the phone is equally as stunning when folded as the screen on any top smartphone. It's made for short tasks like texting back and forth, utilizing Google Assistant, and even snapping selfies with the back camera without having to unfold the smartphone. Like Google's non-folding smartphones, this external screen is bright and sharp while keeping the same high quality.

The inner screen is the star of the show when unfolds. With an adjustable refresh rate of up to 120Hz and HDR support, it's not just big it's exquisitely made. This implies that everything you see will be silky smooth, including scrolling online pages and high-definition films. By automatically decreasing the rate when more performance is not required, the adaptive refresh rate also contributes to battery conservation.

Sunlight visibility is also adjusted for the display. The Super Actua Flex technology, which is exclusive to Google, keeps the screen bright and clear even in direct sunlight. You won't need to look for shade or strain your eyes to access your material, whether you're working outside or just browsing on the go.

Using the Fold Mechanism Safely

For new users of foldable gadgets, one of the main problems is learning how to operate the fold mechanism safely and efficiently. Although the Pixel 9 Pro Fold has an innovative hinge that makes folding the phone feel natural, there are still certain best practices and maintenance tips to remember.

First, instead of pulling from the edges, always open and close the gadget from the middle of the screen. Because the hinge can take tension when it is spread properly, folding with your thumb in the center will guarantee that the mechanism functions smoothly and uniformly over time. When using the device for an extended period, forcing it open from the edges may put undue strain on the hinge and result in damage.

To shield the foldable design of the Pixel 9 Pro Fold from dirt, dust, and moisture, Google has included protective layers. It's still advised to stay away from using the device in extremely moist or dusty conditions, though. Particles becoming stuck inside the hinge can interfere with its smooth functioning and eventually cause the interior parts to deteriorate. To keep the screen and hinge clear of debris, it is advised to clean them regularly with a microfiber cloth.

HARDWARE OVERVIEW AND DEVICE LAYOUT

The flexible durability of the Pixel 9 Pro Fold is among its most comforting features. The hinge has undergone extensive testing by Google and is designed to withstand thousands of folds without losing its flexibility. But, like with any precise part, the longevity of the hinge can be greatly increased by careful management. Aim to avoid opening the device too soon when unfolding it. Use a steady motion instead, as it is kinder to the internal machinery and feels more fulfilling.

It's critical to remember that compared to conventional glass screens, foldable displays are more sensitive. Even though Google designed it to be durable, users should still refrain from applying too much pressure to the foldable screen. If the gadget needs to be kept in a purse or pocket, be sure nothing sharp could scratch the screen.

These easy instructions will guarantee that the folding mechanism stays in top shape and give you years of trouble-free use.

The first step to realizing the full potential of the Google Pixel 9 Pro Fold is to become proficient with its hardware and physical layout. From the sophisticated foldable design to the natural arrangement of buttons and ports, every component has been developed with the user experience in mind. By using the folding mechanism responsibly, you can preserve the best features that contemporary smartphone technology has to offer while also keeping your device in excellent condition.

4

Using the Pixel 9 Pro Fold to navigate Android 14

Combining the capability of Android 14 with the power of Google's most recent hardware, the Pixel 9 Pro Fold is a technological marvel. This tablet has a sophisticated, user-friendly interface that is optimized for its folding form factor, making it an immersive experience to navigate. The principles of Android 14 as it functions on the Pixel 9 Pro Fold will be examined in this chapter, with particular attention paid to three important topics: Home Screen Basics and Customization; Navigation Gestures and Quick Settings; and Exploring the Fold-Specific Interface.

Basics of the Home Screen and Customization

Your command center on the Pixel 9 Pro Fold is the home screen. With Android 14, users can interact with their home screen much better, especially when utilizing the foldable design. The home screen greets you as soon as you unlock the phone, bringing you into an elegant yet comfortable world where widgets, apps, and important data coexist.

Simple Layout

The Pixel 9 Pro Fold's home screen has a simple design when it first powers on. Your most used apps, including the phone, browser, and camera, are easily accessible from the dock at the bottom of the screen, and a status bar with the time, battery life, and Wi-Fi signal is located at the top of the screen. More room for icons is provided by the large display, which facilitates easy app organization and access without looking cluttered.

Personalizing Your Home Display

One of the main features of Pixel is personalization. With Android 14, you may fully customize your home screen. To begin, press and hold any vacant space on the screen. A menu with the ability to modify the home screen layout, wallpaper, widgets, and theme will then show up.

1. Themes and Wallpapers

Dynamic wallpapers on the Pixel 9 Pro Fold offer a distinctive visual experience by adjusting to the lighting in your surroundings. Pick from a variety of static or moving wallpapers to suit your taste. Additionally, you may alter the theme by choosing colors that correspond with your wallpaper, which Android 14 applies to the entire device. This provides a unified appearance throughout your alerts, settings, and home screen.

2. Technology

Another useful tool on the home screen is widgets. Android 14 features increased widget capability, enabling interactive widgets that can display current information, such as weather updates, calendar events, and even AI-powered suggestions based on your activities. To move a widget onto your display, long-press the home screen, select "Widgets," and then drag the desired widget. With the Pixel 9 Pro Fold's bigger screen, there is more space for widget placement without feeling crowded.

3. Setting Up Apps

The Pixel 9 Pro Fold has a very intuitive app rearranging. To keep your workspace organized, drag and drop apps into folders or between multiple home screens. To make apps easier to find when you need them, you may even group them according to their purpose or usage. It is particularly helpful for multi-page home screens because of its foldable screen, which lets you set apart distinct areas for work, media, or everyday necessities.

4. Google Find Out

You can access Google Discover by swiping right from the main home screen. Here, you can get news, articles, and updates that are customized based on your interests. With Google Discover, Android 14 guarantees a more seamless and responsive experience that instantly adjusts to your preferences.

Quick Settings and Navigation Gestures

With an emphasis on smoothness and usability, Android 14 has improved navigation gestures to match the design and capabilities of the Pixel 9 Pro Fold. You can become proficient with your Pixel's navigation system by learning gestures that, once mastered, will replace conventional on-screen buttons.

Basics of Gesture Navigation

The Pixel 9 Pro Fold's immersive gesture-based navigation technology does away with the necessity for buttons. Below is a summary of the main gestures:

1. Home Gesture: Swiping up from the bottom of the screen sends you to the home screen, regardless of the app you're in.

2. Back Gesture: To return to the previous screen or application, swipe inward from the left or right sides of the screen. The Pixel 9 Pro Fold in particular benefits from Android 14's improved gesture responsiveness, which makes the activity fluid even while alternating between open and folded modes.

3. App Switcher: To use the app switcher, swipe up and hold the center of the screen. This allows you to see every app that is open at the moment and select which one to use. You can see more apps at once on the bigger screen, which makes it easier for you to switch between jobs quickly.

4. Split-Screen Gesture: The foldable design substantially improves the ability to enter split-screen mode by long-pressing the app icon in the switcher. Multitasking is easy and effective when you can utilize two programs side by side. For example, you can play a YouTube video on one half of the screen while checking your email on the other.

Short Settings

Android 14's Quick Settings have been revamped for efficiency and ease of use. The Quick Settings menu, which provides toggles for frequently used functions like Wi-Fi, Bluetooth, Do Not Disturb, and brightness adjustment, can be accessed by swiping down from the top of the screen.

- **Customization:** By tapping the pencil symbol at the bottom of the Quick Settings panel, you can change which toggles show up. Toggle your preferred toggles around for easier access.
- **Advanced Features:** When the Pixel 9 Pro Fold is unfolded, you can rapidly choose between using the bigger inner screen and the smaller front display thanks to fold-specific quick settings, like display mode options.

Notifications Administration

Better, more engaging notifications are a feature of Android 14. Notifications can be expanded or interacted with directly from the notification bar in the form of cards. For instance, you can manage media playing from the notification shade or respond to a message without fully launching the app. Notifications are more effectively spaced on the foldable screen, making it simpler to read and reply to them.

Examining the Interface That Is Specific to Folding

A unique interface designed especially for foldable technology makes the Pixel 9 Pro Fold an excellent choice for anybody seeking a dynamic and adaptable experience. When the phone is folded, it functions as a small device with an external display; when it is unfolded, the larger screen makes the Pixel resemble a small tablet.

Being Used to the Fold

Apps seamlessly switch between folded and unfolded modes, according to the screen size automatically. Apps open on the front screen of the phone automatically expand to fill the internal display when you turn it on. For example, unfolding the phone will instantly provide a larger, more immersive viewing experience if you're watching a video on the front display.

Optimization of Multiple Displays

Android 14 improves by using foldable smartphones with multiple displays. You may use the Pixel 9 Pro Fold to run multiple apps simultaneously. For example, you could use one half of the screen for reading an article and the other for taking notes. The versatile style allows apps to change fluidly across displays, offering optimal use for varied tasks.

Continuity of Task

Foldables have a property called task continuity. You don't become disoriented while alternating between the unfolded and folded modes. Android 14 guarantees a seamless transition, keeping everything in place whether you're writing an email or watching a video.

Scroll and Drop

Android 14 makes use of the foldable screen by enabling drag-and-drop capability. For example, you can drag an image from the gallery on one side of the screen and drop it into a message or document on the other. This turns your Pixel into a productivity machine by making multitasking much more natural.

You can fully utilize your Pixel 9 Pro Fold by becoming proficient with the home screen customization, gesture navigation, and the fold-specific interface. With Android 14, the device's everyday convenience and sophisticated multitasking have been specifically improved. Your interaction with this cutting-edge phone becomes smooth and pleasurable when you have these tools at your disposal.

5

Customizing Your Experience with Pixels

More than simply a phone, your Google Pixel 9 Pro Fold is a creative tool, a personal assistant, and an extension of your digital life. Tailoring its look and feel to your preferences and requirements is the greatest approach to making it feel like your device. Managing Notifications and Privacy Settings, Setting Up Widgets and App Layouts, and Customizing Themes and Wallpapers are the three main areas of customization covered in this chapter.

Personalizing Wallpapers and Themes

The look of your phone is among the first things that people notice about it. With the Google Pixel 9 Pro Fold, you have tremendous flexibility to personalize your device by changing its theme and background. These easy-to-make changes can make your phone a reflection of your personality, sense of style, or even how you're feeling at the moment.

Selecting a Wall Covering

Wallpapers are more than simply backdrop graphics; they set the tone for how you feel about your phone. A wide selection of beautiful stock wallpapers, ranging from artistic designs to breathtaking nature photos, are included with the Pixel 9 Pro Fold. To just peruse these choices, navigate to preferences

> Wallpaper & Style in your preferences. If you're not happy with the default settings, you can download a ton of wallpapers from apps like Zedge and Google Wallpapers, or you may look up custom choices online.

But why limit yourself to static photos? Live wallpapers, which can produce a dynamic backdrop experience with subtle movements, are also supported by the Pixel 9 Pro Fold. Live wallpapers have an amazing visual impact, but they could drain your battery a little more. Imagine being able to open your phone and seeing the stars quietly twinkling on a clear night, or calm waves lapping at the shore.

Make your background a picture from your collection for a unique look. Perhaps it's a photo of your loved ones, a recent trip, or even your pet. Your phone gives you a sense of familiarity and connection each time you unlock it.

Looking Into Possible Themes

Using themes, you can alter the Pixel 9 Pro Fold's overall appearance and feel, including the system's colors, fonts, and icons. The Material You design, which dynamically changes your system's color scheme based on your background, is one of Android 14's best features. This implies that your notification shade, quick settings, and even apps will reflect similar tones if you pick a bold, colorful background, giving your phone a unified, visually appealing look.

By navigating to Settings > Wallpaper & Style > Theme, you can further personalize this. Choose the accent and color scheme that best suits your tastes from here. Third-party theme apps, ranging from maximalist to minimalist, are available in the Play Store if you're searching for something a little bolder.

Pro Tip: Google's Pixel 9 Pro Fold offers daily wallpaper rotation, which allows you to change your background automatically every day to keep your phone feeling exciting and new. This is great for people who like to switch things up regularly.

Configuring App Layouts and Widgets

Convenience and functionality are the main goals of widgets and app layouts. They simplify your phone usage and provide quick access to important information. Your Pixel 9 Pro Fold will appear more like you when you customize these components, which also increases efficiency.

Installing and Adapting Widgets

Similar to little apps, widgets are placed on your home screen and offer instant access to particular app features while presenting real-time data. Widgets are an effective way to keep track of everything on the Pixel 9 Pro Fold, including your calendar and weather updates, without having to open separate programs.

Long-press on a space on your home screen, then select Widgets to add a widget. Numerous choices, such as media controls and clock widgets, will be shown to you. Select the one that best fits your needs, then drag and drop it to any location on the home screen.

A widget doesn't have to remain still once it appears on your screen. Certain widgets can be resized, such as At a Glance and the Google Calendar. To change the widget's size or location, long-press on it. This versatility ensures that you may insert as much information as you need, where you need it, without cluttering your home screen.

App Layout Optimization

The way you engage with your phone starts with the arrangement of your home screen. Especially when utilizing the foldable display, the Pixel 9 Pro Fold offers you more real estate than before, therefore it's critical to arrange your apps to optimize accessibility.

De-clutter first. Although it can be tempting to have every app open on the home screen, doing so can make navigating confusing. Rather, organize your frequently used programs into folders. You could make folders labeled "Work," "Social," or "Entertainment," for example, and then arrange relevant apps inside of them. This ensures your favorite apps are always accessible with a single swipe and keeps your home screen tidy.

Consider using the App Drawer more often if you like a more minimalist appearance. It can be accessed by swiping upward from the home screen. In this manner, the remainder of your apps stay hidden and organized, leaving just the widgets and shortcuts that are necessary on the home screen.

Handling Privacy Preferences and Notifications

Notifications have two sides in the modern digital world. They might be overbearing, but they also keep us informed. Acquiring the skill to proficiently handle notifications on your Pixel 9 Pro Fold will aid in maintaining organization and preventing interruptions. Optimizing your privacy settings is essential because your phone contains a lot of sensitive data.

Personalizing Alerts

You have precise control over the notifications you receive and how they show up with the Pixel 9 Pro Fold. Toggle notifications for individual apps under Settings > Notifications to make sure you only see the most critical messages.

Real-time updates are something you might want for apps like texting or email. On the other hand, you can choose to have notifications for infrequently used apps like social media or retail apps displayed silently, so they will appear in your notification tray without disturbing you.

Priority Notifications are another feature of Android 14 that allows you to designate specific contacts or apps as priority senders. Any "Do Not Disturb" settings will be circumvented by these notifications, guaranteeing that you never miss a vital work update or a message from a loved one.

Optimizing Privacy Configurations

Strong privacy controls on your Pixel 9 Pro Fold let you control the data that certain apps and services can access. Go to Settings > Privacy to see the permissions associated with each app.

You have three options for granting access to an application, such as location, camera, or microphone: Allow All the Time, Allow Only While Using the App, or Deny. Additionally, Android 14 has One-Time Permissions, which let an app access particular data just during the current session. This is particularly helpful for apps that shouldn't have ongoing access to private data.

The Privacy Dashboard is another important feature that provides you with a comprehensive overview of the data that your apps are accessing and when. It's an excellent tool to make sure that no app is going over its limitations.

Pro Tip: Use the Pixel 9 Pro Fold's Lockdown Mode to temporarily turn off biometric unlocking features like fingerprint and face unlock. This ensures that only a password can unlock your phone, which is helpful in situations where additional security is required.

You may make your Google Pixel 9 Pro Fold a gadget that not only functions for you but also expresses your unique style by learning how to customize it. Every feature can be customized to improve your experience and everyday workflow, from functional configurations with widgets and notifications to visual adjustments like wallpapers and themes.

6

Understanding the Camera System

With its sophisticated triple camera system and an array of strong and adaptable features, the Google Pixel 9 Pro Fold transforms mobile photography and ranks among the best folding smartphones for both amateur and professional photographers. This chapter will cover the camera's operation, its various specialized settings, and professional advice to help you consistently take beautiful pictures and films.

Triple Camera Setup Overview

The triple camera configuration of the Pixel 9 Pro Fold is engineered to provide unmatched versatility, regardless of the situation: bright light, dim lighting, or close-up detail photography. This arrangement combines:

Main Sensor: This camera features a 50-megapixel (MP) primary sensor that produces crisp, colorful photographs in a range of lighting situations. Its f/1.9 aperture guarantees superior performance in dimly lit environments. Larger sensors also aid in capturing more light, which improves the depth and dynamic range of your images to the level of independent cameras.

Ultra-Wide Camera: Capturing wide-angle scenes or gatherings of people doesn't require you to move farther thanks to this 12-MP ultra-wide camera's

120-degree field of vision. This lens solves the distortion issue that usually befalls wide-angle lenses by keeping clarity even at the frame's boundaries.

Telephoto Lens: With a 5x optical zoom and a 30x Super Res Zoom, this 48-MP telephoto lens sharpens its zoom capabilities. This lens maintains the clarity of details even at extreme magnification, whether you're photographing far-off subjects or require an intense close-up.

Not only is the hardware of these cameras exceptional, but they also seamlessly integrate with Google's state-of-the-art computational photography algorithms. Real-time picture processing and enhancement are made possible by the Pixel 9 Pro Fold's Tensor G4 processor, which collaborates with the camera's software. What was the outcome? Even candid photos have a polished appearance.

Using Extra Modes: Super Res Zoom, Night Sight, and More

Google's proficiency with computational photography is evident in the unique settings available on the Pixel 9 Pro Fold. These options stretch the bounds of smartphone photography, turning difficult shooting situations into chances for breathtaking photos.

Night Sight

The pinnacle of Google's low-light photography is Night Sight. Now more efficient and quicker than before, this mode is available with the Pixel 9 Pro Fold. The days of having to use flash, which frequently warps colors and produces harsh shadows, are long gone. Rather, Night Sight makes use of sophisticated image-stacking technology to combine several quickly shot pictures into a single, bright picture.

Night Sight produces vivid, noise-free photos with astounding detail, even in the darkest settings. The software's ability to automatically adjust exposure levels, shadows, and highlights is the key to producing natural-looking photographs with no work on your part. Photographing a candlelight supper or a nighttime cityscape is much easier with Night Sight, which lets you get pictures that are sometimes even better than what your eyes can see.

High-Resolution Zoom

Since most smartphones use digital zoom, which lowers image quality, zooming on a smartphone has always been challenging. Presenting Super Res Zoom, an AI-powered system that improves your close-up photos without compromising on detail. Super Res Zoom increases the already remarkable 5x optical zoom of the Pixel 9 Pro Fold's telephoto lens to an astounding 30x while preserving image quality.

When the Tensor G4 chip enters the picture, magic happens. Super Res Zoom combines several frames taken at various zoom levels to create a single, high-resolution picture. As a result, the photos are clearer, more detailed, and free of the graininess that is sometimes brought on by excessive magnification. This setting is ideal for photographing wildlife, athletic events, or any other scenario in which getting up close to the subject is not an option.

Other Modes

Portrait Mode: Produce polished portraits by blurring the background slightly and focusing on the subject with a lovely bokeh effect. This setting offers DSLR-like quality by using depth mapping to naturally separate the foreground from the background.

Astrophotography Mode: The Pixel 9 Pro Fold has an astrophotography mode that produces amazing pictures of stars, planets, and even galaxies for individuals who want to capture the night sky. While removing noise, the long exposure setting makes sure that faint stars are visible.

Long Exposure and Action Pan: These settings are intended for artistic motion picture making. Action Pan keeps moving objects crisp while creatively blurring the background, highlighting items like a car or a cyclist. Conversely, long-exposure photography produces amazing light trails and other effects brought forth by moving objects in dimly lit environments.

Guidelines for Getting the Greatest Pictures and Videos

Although the Pixel 9 Pro Fold's technology and software handle a lot of the work, you can improve your photography even more by learning a few tricks. Here are some professional pointers and advice on how to maximize the camera system on your Pixel.

1. Make Use of the Rule of Thirds

Most photographers know the rule of thirds, but it's a lesson that's always worth reiterating. To create a 3x3 grid on your screen, enable the grid lines in your camera settings. For more harmonious and eye-catching images, arrange important components of your composition along these lines or at their intersections.

2. Pay Attention to Lighting

Proper lighting is crucial, even with the Pixel 9 Pro Fold's camera boasting all its computational magic. Make the most of natural light whenever you can, especially in the golden hours (shortly after sunrise or before sunset). Never be afraid to use Night Sight when shooting in difficult lighting settings; it's there to make your life simpler.

3. For Balanced Exposure, Use HDR+

The Pixel's HDR+ technology combines multiple photos taken at various exposures to get the ideal ratio of highlights to shadows. To prevent overexposure and maintain details in both the bright and shadowy parts, turn on this option in high-contrast environments, such as bright outdoor scenes or interiors with strong window light.

4. Play with Perspectives & Angles

Take more than just eye-level pictures. Experiment with different perspectives; get down to the ground for a dramatic shot, or take a higher vantage point to catch a broad picture. With its ultra-wide-angle lens, the Pixel allows you to fit more into the picture without taking a step back, making it ideal for these kinds of artistic endeavors.

5. When in doubt, employ manual focus

Although the Pixel's autofocus is fast and dependable, there are situations in which manual focus can provide you greater control, particularly when taking macro photos or in dimly lit environments. To keep the subject sharp, tap anywhere on the screen to lock focus on that region.

6. Capture Films Using Cinematic Pan

Videographers can create fluid, dramatic videos that resemble professional gimbal shots with the Pixel 9 Pro Fold's Cinematic Pan feature, which slows down footage and stabilizes the camera's movement. Whether you're recording a family moment or a vast landscape, this function gives your recordings a more cinematic feel.

7. Utilize the Editing Tools for Google Photos

Remember to post-process your photo once you've taken it. A variety of image editing options are available in Google Photos, including AI-powered recommendations for improving color, contrast, and brightness. To get the ideal finish, you can also manually adjust specific components in your photographs.

You can take images and films that rival those of a professional photographer with the Google Pixel 9 Pro Fold's sophisticated camera hardware, AI-enhanced software, and these helpful suggestions. This robust camera system has everything you need, regardless of experience level, to produce breathtaking images in any situation.

7

AI Features & Google Assistant

Having a virtual assistant like Google Assistant seamlessly integrated into your smartphone can make life much easier in today's hyper-connected environment. The Google Pixel 9 Pro Fold not only excels in hardware, but its AI capabilities especially through Google Assistant are among the most powerful features available. We'll look at three key areas of using AI and Google Assistant in this chapter: configuring it, utilizing voice commands and smart home connectivity, and leveraging AI to enhance productivity and entertainment.

How to Configure and Use Google Assistant

To fully utilize the AI capabilities of your Google Pixel 9 Pro Fold, you must first set up Google Assistant. This virtual assistant is always available to assist with tasks, provide answers, and manage your smart devices.

Google Assistant Configuration

A straightforward but essential first step in realizing the full potential of your Pixel 9 Pro Fold is setting up Google Assistant. Here's how to configure it:

1. **Begin with the "Hey Google" Setup:** When your Pixel first boots up, you'll be asked to activate Google Assistant. You can always go to Settings >

Apps > Assistant to activate it later if you miss this step. Here, you can alter the "Hey Google" activation phrase or just hit the microphone button on the lock screen or home screen.

2. Customize the Experience: During setup, you will be prompted to record your voice by uttering a few important phrases, so that Google Assistant can learn to match your voice. If you want the Assistant to reply exclusively to you, this guarantees that it will uniquely recognize your voice.

3. Linking Your Accounts: The Google Assistant may be linked to other accounts, such as Spotify, Netflix, or even your home automation system (smart thermostats, Philips Hue lights, Nest thermostats, etc.). It syncs with your Google account. This lets you use voice control to operate a variety of apps and gadgets.

4. Changing Language and Preferences: The Assistant can function in more than one language for multilingual users. To add a supplementary language, just navigate to Assistant Settings> Languages. You may also personalize preferences for things like routines, favorite music services, and news updates.

After setup, Google Assistant turns into a useful ally that you can rely on for assistance with reminders, navigation, and even controlling smart home appliances.

Smart Home Integration and Voice Commands

Google Assistant's integration with voice commands and smart home devices is one of the best features of the Pixel 9 Pro Fold experience. With the help of the Assistant, you can use your phone as a central point for home control, be it lighting, temperature, or music.

Getting the Hang of Voice Orders

Google Assistant's functionality revolves around voice commands, and the Pixel 9 Pro Fold is built to react to your requests quickly and precisely.

Several simple instances are as follows:

General Commands: To begin, say "Hey Google" or "OK Google." Then, follow up with queries like "What's the weather like today?", "Open YouTube," or "Set a timer for ten minutes."

- **Navigation & Directions:** Make use of Google Maps with commands like "Take me home" or "Find the closest coffee shop." The foldable display makes the experience even better with larger map images, and this is especially useful while you're on the go.
- **Communication:** You can send texts, make calls, or even dictate emails. Say, "Let's meet at 7 PM. Send a message to John."

Combining these instructions to create routines is where the real power is found. Say "Good morning," for instance, and the Assistant will turn on the lights, read your daily schedule, and provide you with the latest weather information.

Integrating Smart Homes

The Pixel 9 Pro Fold is a remarkable gadget for controlling smart homes. You can use straightforward voice commands to control anything from appliances to security cameras thanks to support for a broad variety of Internet of Things devices.

Lighting and Thermostats: Saying "Hey Google, turn on the lights" or "Set the temperature to 72 degrees" provides you instant control if you have connected smart lighting or thermostats (like Nest or Philips Hue).

Entertainment Devices: You can use your phone to manage smart TVs or Chromecast by asking it to "Pause the movie" or "Play The Office on Netflix." You can even ask it "What's on my schedule for today?" while the Assistant begins a playlist and lowers the lights in your living room.

Routines are also included in the smart home integration of Google Assistant. For example, you can program a "Good Night" routine that, with a single command, turns off all the lights, locks the doors, and sounds the alarm. The ability to automate chores can greatly improve daily efficiency.

Using AI to Boost Entertainment and Productivity

Google Assistant on the Pixel 9 Pro Fold offers a plethora of AI-driven capabilities that are intended to improve productivity and your entertainment experience, in addition to voice commands and smart home connection.

AI to Boost Productivity

The Pixel 9 Pro Fold, powered by the Tensor G4 chip, pushes AI boundaries, giving a personalized experience for busy professionals and multitaskers.

Real-Time Translation: You can use real-time translation for discussions because Google Translate is integrated into the Assistant. Your Pixel can translate text into more than 40 languages with only a simple "Hey Google, be my interpreter" command. This capability is especially helpful for business trips.

Smart Composing Emails: Google Assistant can offer Smart Reply recommendations while you're writing an email or message. You can even voice-dictate whole emails. This decreases typing time and boosts efficiency when multitasking.

Calendar and Reminders: You can set reminders and manage your calendar with Google Assistant. A straightforward directive such as "What's on my calendar for tomorrow?" or "Remind me to call Sarah at 3 PM" keeps you organized without lifting a finger.

By reducing manual labor and allowing your phone to adjust to your daily needs whether they be communication, scheduling, or navigation you can use AI for productivity.

AI for Entertainment

Google Assistant is an excellent partner for entertainment. The integration of AI with streaming services allows for a hands-free media experience.

Music and Video Control: Without opening an app, ask Google Assistant to play your preferred playlist, adjust the volume, or skip tracks. It is also possible to request particular playlists, artists, or genres. "Select some soothing music" will bring up the right track.

Smart Content Recommendations: Based on your past viewing or listening habits, the Assistant can suggest TV series, films, and songs thanks to AI that learns your tastes. The next time you ask yourself, "What should I watch tonight?" it might recommend movies that are similar to the action ones you've previously viewed."

Interactive and Gaming Features: If you enjoy playing video games on your phone, Google Assistant can open games, log your gameplay, and even offer advice on particular titles. It also incorporates YouTube and other sites to offer tutorials on gaming.

Leveraging AI for entertainment allows you to spend more time enjoying well-curated content that is controlled by simple gestures or your voice, rather than wasting time looking for what you're looking for.

The Pixel 9 Pro Fold's AI and Google Assistant are strong features that can improve your life in a variety of ways. These features are essential to the Pixel experience, ranging from setting up and customizing your Assistant to using voice commands to operating your smart home and entertainment system and utilizing AI to increase your productivity and enjoyment. When you embrace this intelligent technology, your Pixel 9 Pro Fold transforms from a phone into an important helper that makes your life easier.

8

Tools for Productivity and Multitasking

It's essential to maximize smartphone efficiency in the fast-paced digital world of today. With its folding design, the Google Pixel 9 Pro Fold offers a range of productivity and multitasking tools that let users manage tasks, switch between apps, and streamline their workflow. The three main concepts covered in this chapter Split-Screen Mode and App Pairs, Using the Taskbar and Recent Apps Menu, and Optimizing the Foldable Screen for Work and Play are at the heart of this productivity revolution.

App Pairs and Split-Screen Modes

Using the phone's large internal display, split-screen mode on the Google Pixel 9 Pro Fold transforms working across apps at the same time and is more than simply a convenience. This function is perfect for multitasking because it lets you run two apps simultaneously. Split-screen mode improves productivity without requiring you to go between apps, whether you're reviewing papers, watching a video while responding to emails, or taking notes during a video chat.

How to Turn on Split-Screen Viewing

Split-screen mode is surprisingly easy to activate. Open the app that you want to utilize first. To reach the Recent Apps view, swipe up from the bottom of the screen, tap the app icon at the top of the card, and choose Split Screen. You will now be asked to select another app to take up the remaining half of the screen. If more room is needed for one app, you may simply resize the split by moving the divider.

Increased Productivity with App Pairs

App Pairs, an innovative feature on the Pixel 9 Pro Fold, lets you save app combinations that you commonly use together. This allows you to press once to rapidly start two apps in split-screen mode. For example, you can integrate your calendar software with an email app to evaluate appointments while drafting responses. You can construct shortcuts that drastically reduce the time spent opening and arranging apps one by one by saving these pairs.

Split-Screen Mode Use Cases

- **Business:** Examine a contract while participating in a video conference, or open a spreadsheet next to a document to cross-reference data.
- **Entertainment**: Use one window for social media surfing or contacting friends, and the other for watching a video.
- **Learning:** Take notes in a text editor while reading an article or watching a tutorial.
- For jobs that call for both active input and real-time information, like managing social media accounts, trading stocks, or live blogging, split-screen mode is quite helpful.

Making Use of the Recent Apps Menu and Taskbar

One of the most effective multitasking features on the Pixel 9 Pro Fold is the Taskbar, which enables quick access to your favorite apps and seamless task transitions. Whether you're in the middle of working or just surfing the web, the taskbar always stays within reach, making program switching and multitasking easier.

Using the Taskbar Navigation

The taskbar is a permanent feature that appears at the bottom of the screen and displays a row of commonly used apps once it is enabled. The taskbar is visible when you swipe up from the bottom of the screen when working in full-screen mode. From there, you can tap to open an app in full-screen mode or swiftly slide its icon to one side of the screen to enable split-screen functionality. This lets you multitask without letting go of the program you're using at the moment.

Because of the taskbar's great degree of customization, you may choose which apps open instantly. This reduces the amount of time you spend looking through the app drawer by enabling you to always have your most-used productivity apps like email, messaging, and a notes app at your fingertips.

Recent Apps Menu: A Productivity Gem

Apart from the taskbar, you can slide to navigate among your most recently opened apps in the Recent Apps Menu. The Pixel 9 Pro Fold is unique because of this feature's ease of use. You can open numerous programs, see what you've recently accessed, and switch between tasks with ease.

For example, the recent apps menu makes it easy to move between your web browser and a note-taking app while you're working on a project and need to go back to work quickly. To access your recent apps, just slide up; then, press to return to the app you require. It's similar to having several tabs open on your desktop computer, but with mobile optimization.

Use Cases for the Taskbar and Recent Apps Menu

Efficiency: You can complete tasks more quickly and with fewer interruptions to your workflow when you have quick access to your favorite or recently used apps.

Multitasking: Flip between several apps with ease and never lose attention.

Customization: Customizing the taskbar to suit your requirements be they professional, social networking, or recreational improves the user experience.

Making the Foldable Screen Great for Play and Work

With its large folding screen, the Google Pixel 9 Pro Fold is made with productivity in mind, offering the perfect space for work and play. Due to the phone's ability to fully unfold, users can multitask on a mobile device just like on a desktop thanks to the increased screen real estate compared to standard smartphones.

Utilizing Screen Area for Productivity

The Pixel 9 Pro Fold provides a display big enough to resemble a small tablet when fully unfolded, which creates a lot of work opportunities. Picture yourself utilizing a text processor and a research browser in split-screen mode. Alternatively, you could edit a photo with the full-size preview on the right and the app controls on the left. Not only does the foldable screen offer more room, but smarter space as well, with every pixel tailored for increased efficiency.

Customizable Designs for a Smooth Experience

Because the phone's software is designed to be flexible, apps will automatically resize to fit the screen size. The experience of utilizing apps in split-screen or single-screen mode is improved by this flexible layout. For example, chat applications make it simpler to read and reply to lengthy discussions, while email apps automatically adjust to display more of your inbox.

Entertainer's Game-Changer

The folding screen is as brilliant when playing. The huge internal display makes streaming and gaming on mobile devices more engaging. The wide perspective of the display gives gamers more control and information, and for movie buffs, it provides an immersive, cutting-edge cinematic experience without requiring a tablet or other external device.

TOOLS FOR PRODUCTIVITY AND MULTITASKING

Cases for Enhancing the Foldable Display

- **Remote Work:** Turn your phone into a tiny workstation during travel. Access a presentation and use a video conference to discuss points with a colleague.
- **Content Creation:** Using the extra space on the foldable screen for a more upscale appearance, editing images, creating graphics, or even overseeing video changes.
- **Streaming and Gaming:** Unwind with widescreen video material that resembles a little tablet, or enjoy improved visuals and control layouts for gaming.

The integration of advanced productivity and multitasking functions in the Google Pixel 9 Pro Fold redefines the way people interact with their smartphones. Whether you want to optimize the foldable display for work and pleasure, divide your screen for efficiency, or customize your taskbar for easy access, the Pixel 9 Pro Fold transforms a once-traditional mobile experience into a cutting-edge, productive beast.

9

Advanced Hints and Techniques

We will delve further into sophisticated features in this chapter to help you realize the full potential of your Google Pixel 9 Pro Fold. These cutting-edge tips and tricks will improve your Pixel experience, whether you're a tech fanatic hoping to tweak every feature of your gadget or just seeking to get more battery life out of it. We'll look at developer settings and hidden features, performance and energy optimization techniques, and how to become proficient with gestures and shortcuts for faster usage.

Developer Options and Hidden Features

Beneath its elegant exterior, the Google Pixel 9 Pro Fold is a powerhouse of functionality, with some of the most potent tools nestled in the Developer Options. To improve the performance of your device, this section will walk you through turning on these options and taking advantage of some of the greatest hidden capabilities.

How to Turn on Developer Preferences:

Developer Mode must be enabled before using developer tools; it is hidden by default to avoid unintentional changes.

1. Navigate to About Phone by scrolling down from Settings.

ADVANCED HINTS AND TECHNIQUES

2. Press and hold "Build Number" seven times. A prompt stating that you are now a developer will appear.

3. Go back to Settings > Scroll down to find Developer Options at the bottom of the list.

When you're in Developer Options, you have a ton of tools at your disposal:

Force Dark Mode: Not many apps support Google's dark mode natively, but it's a terrific way to save battery life and lessen eye strain. You may force dark mode on apps that don't have this feature enabled by going into Developer Options.

Window Animation Scale: Change the window and transition animation scale from 1x to 0.5x to shorten the time spent on transitions. This reduces the amount of time that is spent on visual transitions, making your device feel substantially faster.

USB Debugging: This is a must for anyone who likes to play around with or sideload apps. This enables you to test, root, or perform advanced troubleshooting on your Pixel by connecting it to a computer.

Mock Location: This feature lets you imitate various GPS locations, which is ideal for testing navigation functions or even for playing location-based games with a twist if you're a developer or just testing location-based apps.

Force 90Hz Refresh Rate: To conserve battery life, the dynamic display of the Pixel 9 Pro Fold alternates between refresh rates on its own. To provide a flawless and fluid experience, it is recommended to permanently set the refresh rate to 90Hz to achieve smooth animations and seamless scrolling.

You can adjust the background process limit and device optimization for particular workloads in the developer options, which enables you to customize your Pixel's performance to meet your requirements.

Performance Enhancements and Battery Optimization

One of the most important aspects of smartphone performance is battery life, and the Pixel 9 Pro Fold offers a lot of capabilities for optimizing battery efficiency. With a dual-battery setup, foldable display, and power-hungry apps, you'll want to maximize each charge.

Adjustable Voltage and Power Supply:
  With Adaptive Battery, the Pixel 9 Pro Fold leverages machine learning to give your most-used apps top priority while reducing background activity for apps you don't often use. It learns your habits over time and becomes more efficient with battery use. Here's how to make it active:

1. Go to Battery in the Settings.
2. Toggle on Adaptive Battery by tapping on it.

Adaptive Charging is an essential feature that helps maintain long-term battery health by charging your phone more gradually during the night and only reaching 100% by the time you wake up.

Mode for Battery Saving:
  Although Battery Saver has long been a standard feature, the Pixel 9 Pro Fold improves upon it with the addition of Extreme Battery Saver, which restricts practically everything but for necessary services. If you're in a hurry, this can prolong battery life by many hours:

1. Go to Battery in the Settings.
2. Toggle Extreme Battery Saver on after selecting Battery Saver.

Minimum Background Input:
  Your battery may be gradually depleted by background-running apps without you ever noticing. For specific apps, you can manually restrict or turn off background processes:

1. Open Apps > See All Apps from Settings.
2. After tapping on the disputed app, choose Battery.
3. Make the selection Restricted to stop background activity.

Performance Enhancement with Power Preferences:
Power Preferences can also be configured with the Pixel 9 Pro Fold device. Within the settings, you may divide the available resources between high performance, which is ideal for multitasking and gaming, and a more power-efficient option that uses less energy when performing less demanding tasks.

1. Select Battery > Battery Saver under Settings.
2. After selecting Set Schedule, adjust it according to your usage habits.

Use the built-in monitoring tool to keep an eye on battery-draining apps and modify or remove any that use excessive amounts of power. Your Pixel will constantly operate at maximum efficiency thanks to this proactive management, all without significantly reducing battery life.

Making Effective Use of Gestures and Shortcuts

Using shortcuts and gestures to navigate the Pixel 9 Pro Fold can drastically improve your daily smartphone experience. Once you get the hang of them, these tools can greatly increase your productivity by making it easier for you to access features, apps, and settings.

Simple Navigation Motions:
Gesture-based navigation, which helps simplify multitasking and ordinary phone use, is fully supported by the Pixel 9 Pro Fold. Here are some fundamental motions:

To access the home screen, swipe up from the bottom **(Swipe Up)**.
Swipe Up and Hold to open the menu of recently used apps.

Swipe Left or Right to swiftly navigate between apps on the navigation bar.

It's worth taking some time to get acclimated to gesture navigation if you're used to traditional buttons because it's a quicker and more natural way to operate your phone.

Short Motions:

Fast gestures are a hallmark of the Pixel series. These are intended for time-saving, basic tasks:

- **Double Tap to Wake:** To wake your device, simply tap the screen twice. With foldable phones, where the power button may not always be easily accessible, this is very helpful.
- **Flip to Shhh:** To enter Do Not Disturb mode when in a meeting or needing to concentrate, just flip your phone face down.

Active Edge: Pressing the phone's sides may activate the Google Assistant on some models. This is a useful shortcut to use your device without using your hands.

Higher Level Shortcuts:

Quick Camera Access: You can guarantee you never miss a shot by double-pressing the power button to rapidly open the camera.

Split-Screen Multitasking: You can easily switch to split-screen mode by dragging an app to the top or bottom of the screen after swiping up and holding to access recent apps. This is especially helpful with the huge folding display of the Pixel 9 Pro Fold.

Context Menus and App Shortcuts:

Contextual shortcuts are shown by long-pressing an app icon. For example, to obtain directions to your house or place of employment fast, long-press the Google Maps symbol. With the help of this feature, you may navigate more quickly and easily access frequently used features without having to open the program.

Accessibility Gestures:

Enabling Accessibility Gestures allows you to operate a lot of the device without ever looking at the screen. For example, you can use accessibility touch to pinch-to-zoom or swipe from the corner to engage Google Assistant.

Gaining proficiency with these undiscovered functions, battery enhancements, and gesture controls turns your Google Pixel 9 Pro Fold into an efficient work machine. These sophisticated tips and tricks will help you get the most out of your Pixel experience, whether your goals are to increase battery life, optimize performance, or navigate more quickly using gestures and shortcuts.

10

Features of Accessibility

The Google Pixel 9 Pro Fold is engineered to be a universally accessible device that meets the requirements of all users, irrespective of their physical capabilities. Making cell phones user-friendly for folks with disabilities or those who might need to make changes to their device's settings to use them comfortably depends on accessibility features. We explore the key accessibility features offered by the Pixel 9 Pro Fold below, including activating and personalizing accessibility settings, voice access, talkback, and magnification, and tuning the device for older users and those with disabilities.

Activating and Tailoring Accessibility Features

Numerous simple-to-use, built-in accessibility features are available in Google's Pixel series, which includes the Pixel 9 Pro Fold. Whether you are a seasoned smartphone user with particular accessibility requirements or you are brand-new to the Pixel, personalizing the device to meet your needs is simple and powerful.

Setting Up Accessibility Features

It's easy to start using the Accessibility menu. Navigate to Settings, then scroll down to the Accessibility option. A variety of tools and options are

FEATURES OF ACCESSIBILITY

available in this menu that have the power to completely change the way you use your device. These environments accommodate a range of demands, including vision impairments, hearing impairments, and motor difficulties.

To make the on-screen content easier to read for users with low vision or color blindness, the Pixel 9 Pro Fold offers a user-friendly walkthrough when you first enable accessibility features. This walkthrough guides you through options like text size adjustment, high contrast modes, and color inversion. Moreover, users can enlarge text and icons using the Display Size setting, making the device's interface more user-friendly for elderly or visually impaired people.

Adjusting for Particular Requirements

Customizing the accessibility tools on the Pixel 9 Pro Fold is where its true strength lies. For example, Color Correction is accessible to users who are color blind, and you can select from various filters, such as Tritanomaly or Protanomaly, based on your requirements. For multimedia content, you may also activate subtitles and change the style and size of the subtitles to make them easier to read.

Audio Adjustment is another important function that enables people with hearing impairments to adjust audio balance or boost specific sound frequencies. Mono audio, for instance, makes sure that both channels can be heard through an earphone or speaker for people who have trouble hearing in one ear. For those with hearing impairments, this feature along with configurable vibration alerts is essential.

Easy Access to Features for Accessibility

The Pixel 9 Pro Fold lets users customize accessibility shortcuts for fast and simple access to key settings. Streamlining the experience without requiring considerable menu navigation, features like Magnifier, TalkBack, or Voice Access may be used instantaneously by assigning a gesture (such as hitting both volume buttons) or adding a shortcut to the home screen.

TalkBack, Magnification, and Voice Access

With features like Voice Access, TalkBack, and Magnification, Google has made great progress in producing accessible smartphones. As a result, the Pixel 9 Pro Fold is an incredibly responsive and adaptive tool for anyone with physical or sensory difficulties.

Audio Connection

Voice Access on the Pixel 9 Pro Fold gives users who want a hands-free experience or have motor impairments complete control over the device using voice commands. This feature, which can be enabled via Settings > Accessibility > Voice Access, is revolutionary. After it's configured, users can start using Voice Access by saying, "Hey Google, start Voice Access," and can operate the phone without ever touching it.

Voice Access allows users to browse between screens, open apps, and even dictate text messages. It integrates with the UI and apps with ease. On-screen components are given numbers by the system, so uttering commands like "tap 3" will result in the pushing of a button. Furthermore, it understands normal language, so users may say "scroll down," "go home," or "open Gmail" to complete basic operations.

You can also use the power of Voice Access for certain actions. For example, users can take pictures, switch between Wi-Fi and volume, and modify the latter, which makes it a great choice for people who have mobility issues.

TalkBack

TalkBack is a crucial function for users who are blind or have low vision. When TalkBack is enabled (Settings > Accessibility > TalkBack), it speaks feedback during each interaction and narrates what is seen on screen. TalkBack says aloud the selections you make as you swipe or tap the screen, giving you confidence to confidently use the device.

FEATURES OF ACCESSIBILITY

TalkBack has customized gestures that let users conduct activities by swiping, double-tapping, or holding particular regions of the screen. By providing an effective method of reading messages, using apps, and browsing the web without relying on eyesight, this functionality empowers blind individuals.

The fact that TalkBack connects with Google Assistant and other apps to offer a seamless phone experience is particularly useful. For instance, users can use voice commands to instruct Google Assistant to start apps, read texts, or transmit messages in their entirety. TalkBack facilitates these actions.

Magnification

Users who have low vision will find the Magnification tool to be extremely helpful. With the help of this tool, users can utilize gestures to zoom in on any area of the screen. Users can enlarge text, photos, and icons by triple-tapping the screen to activate Magnifier.

Users can also choose to have a floating magnification window that they can drag around the screen in addition to full-screen magnification. Users can zoom in on particular areas of the screen using this window that resembles a magnifying glass without losing sight of the interface as a whole.

This function is highly helpful for regular browsing or app use, especially when combined with additional features like high contrast text or dark mode, which lessen eye strain while maintaining legible information.

Device Optimization for Elderly and Handicapped Users

In addition to being a cutting-edge technological device, the Pixel 9 Pro Fold is made with everyone in mind, including the elderly and the disabled. Google has included considerate features that are easily customizable, making the phone fun and accessible for individuals who might find it overwhelming or challenging to utilize modern technology.

Simplified Senior User Experience

The foldable screen of the Pixel 9 Pro Fold adds a big benefit for elders. The wide display provides greater space when unfolded, allowing users to browse and read text without squinting or straining to see smaller symbols. You may minimize eye strain by adjusting the Display Size and Text Size settings to make everything from contact lists to text messages easier to read.

Enabling gesture navigation simplifications (e.g., larger touch targets, no swipe-based commands) can make the phone considerably easier to use for people who are not experienced with touch gestures or sophisticated UI features. Thanks to the Pixel Launcher's many customization options, users can arrange their preferred apps for easy access on the home screen.

Particular Resources for Individuals with Impairments

Additionally, the Pixel 9 Pro Fold comes with several pre-configured accessibility shortcuts for those with disabilities. For instance, from the lock screen or home screen, users with motor impairments can instantly use Voice use or Switch Access.

For people who are hard of hearing, Hearing Assistance technologies like Live Transcribe and Sound Amplifier offer real-time speech-to-text translation. These functions make it possible for users to have conversations without the need for hearing aids, which is especially helpful in loud settings or during meetings.

FEATURES OF ACCESSIBILITY

Switch Access gives users of wheelchairs or people with restricted mobility the ability to operate the phone via external switches (such as Bluetooth headsets or other gear), giving them even more options for controlling the phone without touching the screen.

The Pixel 9 Pro Fold is a smartphone that prioritizes inclusivity, providing a range of customizable accessibility features to cater to the varied demands of its users. It is much more than just a technological marvel. Google has made sure that every user, regardless of age or ability, can enjoy a seamless and empowering smartphone experience with features like Voice Access and TalkBack.

11

Maintenance and Troubleshooting

Although having a high-end gadget like the Google Pixel 9 Pro Fold might be an incredible experience, not everything in technology is flawless. This chapter will address frequent problems that users could run into and offer workable fixes, with an emphasis on folding screens and battery maintenance. To keep you informed, we'll cover the crucial procedures for backing up and resetting your device. This section will provide you with the information to confidently address any potential issues and keep your Pixel 9 Pro Fold in perfect condition, regardless of your level of experience with smartphones.

Typical Problems and Their Fixes

The Google Pixel 9 Pro Fold, like every smartphone, may occasionally have bugs or malfunctions despite its state-of-the-art design. This is a guide to the most common problems and their fixes.

1. Unresponsive Screen

The most frequent annoyance experienced by smartphone users is a slow or unresponsive screen. This can feel like a more urgent problem with a foldable tablet. Try a soft reset by holding down the power button for approximately

MAINTENANCE AND TROUBLESHOOTING

ten seconds if you find that the Pixel 9 Pro Fold screen is not responding. This restarts the device and fixes the majority of short-term issues. Make sure you have the most recent version of your program installed since Google frequently provides patches to address known bugs.

2. Overly Rapid Battery Drain

The Pixel 9 Pro Fold naturally uses a lot of energy because of its powerful specifications and huge display. Rapid drainage, though, can point to a problem with a background activity. Examine the apps that are consuming the most battery first:

- To find out which apps are consuming your battery, go to Settings > Battery > Battery usage.
- Turn on Battery Saver, disable pointless background programs, and make sure brightness is set to auto-adjust.
- Try recalibrating the battery by letting it discharge completely and then charging it to 100% if it is still draining unusually quickly.

3. Freezing and Crashes in Apps

Apps can abruptly crash or freeze at times. The most expedient approach to remedy this is to remove the app's cache:

- Choose the app that's giving you trouble by going to Settings > Apps > All apps, then press Clear cache.

Reinstall the app after uninstalling it if the problem still exists. If several apps crash frequently, it can indicate a more serious software problem that can be fixed with a phone restart or system upgrade.

4. Wi-Fi Connectivity Issues

If your Pixel 9 Pro Fold is failing to stay connected to Wi-Fi or won't connect at all, try the following steps:

Turn on and off the Wi-Fi.

- Tap your network and choose Forget after forgetting the network and reconnecting: Settings > Network & internet > Wi-Fi.
- Try connecting to a different network or restarting your router. Resetting your network settings (Settings > System > Reset options > Reset Wi-Fi, mobile & Bluetooth) may be helpful in extreme circumstances.

5. Heating Problems

Another frequent problem is overheating, particularly when utilizing resource-intensive apps like gaming or streaming videos. Although the Pixel 9 Pro Fold's sophisticated cooling technology reduces this, in the unlikely event that you overheat:

- Turn off the phone's charge, end all open apps, and let it cool.
- Try to use apps in a more comfortable setting.
- Checking the Battery usage page to verify if an app is running excessively is a smart idea, as overheating can also be an indication of excessive background processes.

Taking Care of the Battery and Foldable Screen

The folding screen of the Pixel 9 Pro Fold is one of its most distinctive and delicate characteristics. Even though Google made this extremely sturdy, it still needs to be properly cared for to last a long time. Let's talk about optimal practices for the battery and the foldable display.

1. Care for Foldable Screens

Although the foldable screen is an engineering wonder, it needs special handling to prevent damage:

Avoid excessive pressure: Take care not to apply too much pressure to the screen, particularly in the area close to the fold. Even though the screen is meant to be flexible, using too much effort could break it.

Regular cleaning: The fold or hinge may collect dust and tiny particles. Frequently wipe the screen with a gentle microfiber cloth. Use of strong chemicals or high moisture content should be avoided as they could leak into the hinge mechanism.

Use a case: A case made specifically to shield your Pixel 9 Pro Fold from dings and scratches won't interfere with its ability to fold. Steer clear of third-party accessories that can strain the screen or hinge.

2. Upkeep of Batteries

The high-capacity battery that comes with the Pixel 9 Pro Fold can be extended by following these suggestions:

Avoid severe temperatures: The lifespan and performance of batteries can be impacted by heat and cold. Keep your phone out of the freezing or bright sunshine.

- Charge mindfully: The idea that you should wait to charge your phone after completely draining it is untrue. Charging a battery between 20% and 80% can assist in maintaining its health over time.
- Activate Adaptive Battery: This function learns your usage patterns and limits power to programs you don't frequently use to maximize battery efficiency. Go to Settings > Battery > Adaptive Battery and turn it on.

3. Caution with Hinges

Since the hinge is essential to the folding design, adequate maintenance will guarantee that it functions smoothly:

- Open and close gently: Steer clear of forcefully opening or shutting the phone. Although the hinge is designed to be flexible, it should be handled carefully.

Dust prevention: Although the hinge is made to withstand dust infiltration, it's still a good idea to keep the phone out of sandy or unclean areas for extended periods.

Backing up and resetting your device

Occasionally, a more radical approach is required to get your device operating again, particularly if troubleshooting hasn't been able to address persistent problems. As a last option, you may choose to reset your Pixel 9 Pro Fold, but before you do, make sure you know the difference between a factory and a soft reset and how to properly back up your data.

1. Soft Reset

A soft reset is simply rebooting the phone without losing data. When addressing minor issues like app crashes or unresponsiveness, you should start with these:

- Hold the power button for 10-15 seconds until the screen shuts off, then power the device back on. This fixes a lot of problems and frees up the system's temporary memory without compromising your personal information.

2. Reset by Factory

Your phone is returned to its initial configuration after a factory reset erases all of its data. This is helpful if you're planning to sell the gadget or are addressing ongoing problems:

System > Reset options > Erase all data (factory reset) under Settings.

Make sure you back up all crucial data before doing a factory reset (more on that below). Keep in mind that doing this will remove all settings, programs, and files.

3. Creating Data Backups

By backing up your Pixel 9 Pro Fold, you can be sure that crucial data won't

MAINTENANCE AND TROUBLESHOOTING

be lost in the event of a device switch or factory reset. Fortunately, Google simplifies this process:

- Toggle Backup by Google One by going to Settings > Google > Backup . This backs up contacts, settings, call logs, app data, and more.

By turning on Backup & sync in the app's settings, you may also use Google Photos to back up your images and videos independently. Take into consideration using USB to transfer files to your computer for larger files or local backups.

It doesn't have to be difficult to maintain your Google Pixel 9 Pro Fold and deal with frequent problems. You can maintain the optimal condition of both the foldable screen and battery for many years to come by adhering to the above troubleshooting techniques and care advice for your device.

12

Commonly Asked Questions

Owning a Google Pixel 9 Pro Fold can feel like walking into the future with its cutting-edge foldable technology and AI-powered capabilities. Even though the user interface of this phone is meant to be intuitive, there may be circumstances in which you will require assistance to fully utilize it. In addition to answering some of the most common queries from Pixel owners, this chapter provides insightful advice on how to get the most out of your gadget. Now let's get started!

Responses to Frequently Asked Questions

Q1: On my Pixel 9 Pro Fold, how can I enable Face Unlock or Fingerprint Unlock?

First, navigate to Settings > Security on your device to enable Face Unlock or Fingerprint Unlock. Both unlocking techniques are available under the Device Security section. To register your face or fingerprint, adhere to the on-screen instructions. For optimal accuracy while utilizing Face Unlock, make sure you're in a well-lit environment. Fingerprint Unlock operates by simply pressing your finger flat against the sensor. Pixel's Face Unlock combines with other techniques, like as PIN or pattern unlock, for additional protection, guaranteeing a compromise between ease of use and security.

COMMONLY ASKED QUESTIONS

Q2: How can I get the most out of my Pixel 9 Pro Fold's battery?

The Tensor G4 chip, which powers the Pixel 9 Pro Fold, is one of its best features: it can save battery life. Enable Adaptive Battery under Settings > Battery > Adaptive preferences to get the most out of your battery. This AI-powered function learns how you use apps and adjusts battery life for infrequently used apps. Additionally, when your battery is getting low, you can activate Battery Saver mode, which limits background activity and lowers screen brightness. Furthermore, you may prolong the life of your battery by making effective use of the foldable display (avoid prolonged use of the brightest option) and monitoring power-intensive apps.

Q3: Can I change the way my Pixel 9 Pro Fold displays notifications?

Of course! Numerous customization options are available for notifications on Pixel phones. To modify the way that notifications appear on your screen, navigate to Settings > Notifications. You may adjust which apps have priority over others, whether sensitive content should be hidden, and whether they are displayed on the lock screen. Notification Dots are another feature that the Pixel 9 Pro Fold offers. By adding tiny dots to app icons, you can see whether there are any pending notifications.

You may plan downtime or set exceptions for specific contacts and apps using the Do Not Disturb function, which can be accessed from Settings > Sound & vibration > Do Not Disturb. This feature allows for greater customization.

Q4: What should I do if I can't touch the screen on my Pixel 9 Pro Fold?

Make sure the device isn't dirty or wet before proceeding if your screen stops responding. Simple smudges or dust can occasionally cause touchscreen interference. Should that not be the case, attempt restarting your device by choosing Restart while holding down the power button. Whether the problem persists, try starting your phone in Safe Mode to see whether it's related to any third-party apps. By holding down the Power Off button and choosing Safe Mode when requested, you can put your device in safe mode. If none of these fixes resolve the issue, you might need to reset the display calibration via the settings or get in touch with Google support for more help.

Q5: How can I multitask with the foldable screen?

Multitasking is made possible by the huge, folding display of the Pixel 9 Pro Fold. To activate split-screen mode, launch the desired application and swipe upward to access the Recents screen. Click the icon of the application, and choose Split screen. Select another program to open in parallel with it. With the help of this feature, you may browse the web and check your email while conversing with friends or viewing a video. Additionally, App Pairs are supported by the device, which enables you to make shortcuts to commonly used app combinations so you can start them quickly in split-screen mode.

Q6: What's the ideal way to shoot pictures with the Pixel 9 Pro Fold?

With its triple rear camera system, the Pixel 9 Pro Fold offers cutting-edge AI improvements. Try modes like Night Sight for low light and Super Res Zoom for sharp close-ups to take beautiful pictures. When taking pictures of individuals, especially children, the new Made You Look feature is meant to draw their attention and make sure they are looking directly into the camera. Try Macro Focus for close-ups and Portrait mode for images with lots of depth for optimal results. The enhanced front camera now features Face Unlock, which automatically composes the ideal frame for your selfie.

Q7: How can I resolve performance problems?

The first thing to do if your Pixel 9 Pro Fold starts to slow down or lag is to clear your cache. To clear some space, go to Settings > Storage > Cache. Restarting the device regularly is another smart technique that can help with small problems. If issues continue, go to Settings > Battery > Battery usage to see if any apps are consuming too much RAM or draining your battery. Apps that appear harmful can be updated or uninstalled. Lastly, confirm that you have the most recent software updates installed. These updates frequently include bug fixes and performance enhancements.

COMMONLY ASKED QUESTIONS

Guidelines for Optimizing Your Pixel 9 Pro Fold

Boost the Tensor G4 Chip's Power

The Pixel 9 Pro Fold's Tensor G4 chip is optimized to maximize AI features and make your phone faster and smarter. Discover AI-powered features like Live convert, which can convert text from any language into conversations in real-time, and Assistant Voice Typing, which enables you to dictate texts fast and precisely, to get the most out of this powerful processor. The Tensor G4 also boosts photo processing, so using advanced camera modes like HDR+ and Motion Mode lets you capture breathtaking, dynamic photographs with no effort.

Use Features Particular to Folds

The foldable display is not simply a design decision; it's a productivity tool. Benefit from drag-and-drop between programs, split-screen multitasking, and the taskbar, which allows you to easily move between your most-used apps. The huge display can be fully extended to become a mini-tablet, which is ideal for working on documents, watching films, or playing immersive games.

Make It More Accessible for a Customized Experience

To enhance accessibility on your Pixel 9 Pro Fold, consider utilizing features such as Live Caption, which offers captions for any media that is now playing on your phone in real-time. Accessibility settings also include larger font options and magnification gestures. Moreover, Quick Tap on the rear of the phone may be customized to launch particular apps or settings, improving accessibility for people with mobility issues.

Remain Current on Software Updates

Google often upgrades its software as part of its effort to make the Pixel experience better. Make sure you activate automatic updates in Settings > System > System update to get the most recent security, performance, and feature upgrades. For example, Gemini AI enhancements boost the multitasking and responsiveness of the device.

Unlock Your Camera's Full Potential

Investigate the Google Camera's advanced settings to improve your shots. To capture the night sky in stunning detail, select the Astrophotography mode and enable RAW+JPEG capture for greater post-processing versatility. To guarantee you're getting the most out of the hardware, keep the Google Camera app updated. Regular upgrades can bring new capabilities.

You can get the most out of your Pixel 9 Pro Fold by using these suggestions and taking care of typical issues. With this phone, every task will be easier to complete and more intuitive because it is made to fit your specific demands.

13

Conclusion and Further Resources

Now that we've completed this tutorial to the Google Pixel 9 Pro Fold, it's time to consider the salient characteristics of this gadget and the advice that will help users get the most out of it. A list of more resources for further study, debugging, and ecosystem mastery of Pixel will also be included in this chapter. These summaries and tools will prepare you for the voyage ahead, regardless of your level of tech expertise.

Summary of Main Features and Advice

1. Leading-Edge Foldable Structure

The Google Pixel 9 Pro Fold is distinguished primarily by its unique foldable design. The device's smooth, fluid-friction hinge mechanism makes it possible for it to open completely flat, making it useful for multitasking as well as daily duties. In addition to giving the Pixel line a futuristic look, this design offers genuine functionality. Regardless of whether they are viewing videos, using an app, or browsing the web, users can fold the device to various angles.

Tip: Never forcefully close the fold; instead, softly push the hinge area. Google's engineers have engineered the hinge to be durable, but treating it with care will prolong the life of this important mechanism.

2. Excellent Actua Flex Screen

With its largest display yet, the Pixel 9 Pro Fold uses Super Actua Flex Display technology to enable seamless transitions between folded and unfolded modes. Excellent one-handed usage is offered by the outside screen, while gaming, video consumption, and multitasking are best suited for the inner display.

Tip: Customize your screen layout when utilizing split-screen mode. Window dragging and resizing guarantees that you take full advantage of the roomy internal display. Additionally, using "Adaptive Brightness" prolongs battery life while maintaining eye comfort.

3. Tensor G4 Chip Power

The Tensor G4 chip, Google's most potent CPU to date, powers the Pixel 9 Pro Fold. Its machine learning and AI task optimization means that it will operate faster and more effectively whether you're gaming, navigating through complicated apps, or handling daily productivity chores. Everyday experiences are improved by the incorporation of AI, from real-time translation to voice recognition.

Tip: The Tensor G4 excels in background task management, such as maximizing battery life when multitasking. Make sure you investigate battery management settings under "Device Care" to adjust how your apps operate and how much power is used.

4. Advanced Camera System

With its triple rear camera system, the Pixel 9 Pro Fold has completely changed the game in mobile photography. With the addition of telephoto and ultra-wide lenses, the 48 MP primary camera produces photographs with astounding clarity and detail. Notable features like "Macro Focus" for up close photos and "Made You Look", an AI-powered function that highlights a topic in a picture while it's being taken, are perfect for capturing small children's attention during a photo session.

Tip: For unique, high-quality photos, manually change the ISO, white balance, and exposure using the "Pro Mode" in the camera settings. Additionally, remember to use the photo editing suite's "Magic Eraser" to get rid of undesired things from your photos.

5. Google Integration Done Right

The Pixel 9 Pro Fold has extensive integration with Google's ecosystem, just like all Pixel phones. To make activities easier, Google Assistant, Google Lens, and intelligent AI-driven suggestions work together. The Tensor G4 chip boosts the Assistant's capabilities, allowing it to accomplish more tasks including managing your smart home devices, finding specific documents, and creating reminders.

Tip: To enable Google Assistant to identify distinct voices within a home, enable "Voice Match". This enables the Assistant to respond with customization for each user, including calendar appointments and customized reminders.

6. Superior Multitasking

True multitasking is made possible by the huge foldable display and the Android 14 operating system. You may effortlessly run two apps side-by-side or pin selected apps to the screen's taskbar for quick access.

Tip: Use the "App Pairs" option to open two favorite apps simultaneously in split-screen mode. This is especially useful for productivity tasks like watching videos while contacting friends or writing an email while using the internet.

7. Improved Features for Accessibility

The Pixel 9 Pro Fold was created by Google with accessibility in mind, making it usable by individuals of different abilities. To meet various needs, the phone comes with a range of accessibility features, such as high-contrast text options, TalkBack, and Voice Access.

Tip: Customize the gadget to your own tastes by examining the "Accessibility" settings. Custom font sizes, gesture navigation, and text-to-speech are just a few of the features that can greatly enhance the overall experience.

Helpful Resources & Additional Reading

Following your exploration of your Google Pixel 9 Pro Fold, here are some helpful links to help you stay informed and solve any problems you might run into. These links offer comprehensive tutorials, discussion boards, and updates to improve your device knowledge and experience.

1. Google Pixel Help Center

Support for Google Pixel may be found at https://support.google.com/pixel.

The Pixel 9 Pro Fold is one of the Google Pixel devices for which this is the official support website. Comprehensive how-to guides, troubleshooting advice, and direct access to help may all be found here.

2. Documentation for Android 14

Features and Synopsis of Android 14: https://developer.android.com/about/versions/14)

You may see the official documentation by clicking this link if you're interested in learning more about the Android 14 OS that runs your Pixel. You may look through updates, compatibility information, and new features for services and apps.

3. Google Community Forums

[https://support.google.com/pixel/community] is the Google Pixel Community Forum.

Many Google Pixel users in this active community exchange solutions, advice, and ideas. It's a terrific location to get advice and knowledge from other users who might have gone through similar difficulties.

CONCLUSION AND FURTHER RESOURCES

4. Pixel Camera Advice

[https://store.google.com/intl/en/pixel/camera-tips] is the Pixel Camera Guide.

Explore the newest camera tips, lessons, and guides for mastering the photography features of the Pixel 9 Pro Fold. This website has all the information you require, whether you're looking for assistance with a particular camera mode or want to learn new skills.

5. Google's official blog

[Polygon News - Google Blog](https://blog.google/products/pixel)

Get the most recent information about Pixel breakthroughs, feature upgrades, and news directly from Google's official blog. It's also a terrific place to find out about upcoming software releases or new Pixel accessories that improve the experience in general.

6. YouTube Guides

[YouTube.com/results?search_query=google+pixel+9+pro+fold+tutorials] (Google Pixel Tutorials)

For visual learners, YouTube offers a choice of lessons on various functions of the Pixel 9 Pro Fold. YouTube offers extensive videos for all skill levels, whether you're seeking sophisticated advice or basic setup guidance.

As you become proficient with the Google Pixel 9 Pro Fold, refer to this guide frequently. This smartphone is a true technological marvel, with features like the camera system, multitasking capabilities, foldable design, and powerful Tensor G4 CPU. You can make the most of your phone by staying informed and resolving any problems with the resources mentioned above. Cheers to your exploration!

Made in the USA
Columbia, SC
01 February 2025